SPOTLIGHT ON SPECIAL EDU
MEDICAL

Contents

Acknowledgements

The author and publishers wish to express their gratitude to the following organisations for their help and support in the writing of this book:

British Diabetic Association
British Epilepsy Association
National Society for Epilepsy
Cystic Fibrosis Trust
National Asthma Campaign
Action for ME
Cancerlink
Cancer Research Campaign
Children's Heart Federation
Down's Syndrome Association

Addresses, contact telephone numbers and helplines of these, and other organisations can be found at the end of this book.

The author would also like to thank the following for their invaluable help in the writing of the final chapter of this book, and in particular for sharing their experiences on the death of a child:

Nancy McArdle, Headteacher, Thomas Wolsey School, Ipswich
Linda Munns, Headteacher, Rushmere Hall CP School, Ipswich
Claire Sanders, Diosesan Education Committee, Ipswich
Helen Thacker, Advisory Teacher for RE, Suffolk County Council, Education

SPOTLIGHT ON

SPECIAL EDUCATIONAL NEEDS:

MEDICAL CONDITIONS

JOY HOMAN

A NASEN Publication

ISBN 0 906730 96 1

Published by NASEN Enterprises Ltd.
NASEN Enterprises is a company limited by guarantee, registered in England and Wales. Company No. 2637438.

Further copies of this book and details of NASEN's many other publications may be obtained from the Publications Department at its registered office: NASEN House, 4/5, Amber Business Village, Amber Close, Amington, Tamworth, Staffs. B77 4RP.
Tel: 01827 311500; Fax: 01827 313005

Cover design by Graphic Images.
Typeset in Times by J. C. Typesetting and printed in the United Kingdom by J. H. Brookes, Stoke-on-Trent.

SPOTLIGHT ON SPECIAL EDUCATIONAL NEEDS:

MEDICAL CONDITIONS

Introduction

Since the *1981 Education Act*, and more recently the *1994 Code of Practice* and *1996 Education Act*, it has become increasingly common, and accepted, that children with special educational needs/disabilities should be educated alongside their peers in mainstream schools. Previously, children with serious medical conditions were frequently educated in schools for children deemed to be 'physically handicapped and delicate'. Thus children with conditions such as asthma, epilepsy, cystic fibrosis were educated in segregated provision where they had access to all the medical and para-medical facilities they needed but not necessarily to a wide-ranging and stimulating education. It could be said that they were educated in a 'disabled' environment.

The improvement in understanding of many of these conditions, the great strides that have been made in management through better medication, and the entitlement of all children to a broad and balanced curriculum, have all contributed to the inclusion of many children with serious, and sometimes life-threatening, conditions in mainstream classes. It is therefore vital that teachers and other school staff are equipped to deal with situations which might arise as a result of a particular medical condition.

This book seeks to provide a reference for teachers on the more common medical conditions likely to be found in mainstream schools. It aims to assist school staff in feeling less anxious and more confident in meeting the challenge in educating such children. Diabetes, epilepsy, cystic fibrosis, asthma, ME, childhood cancers, heart conditions and Downs syndrome will be discussed. The causes, medical and educational implications and management will be explored.

Much of the information in this book has been drawn from the wealth of literature available from the voluntary organisations which support parents and carers and children. When seeking further information and support, their help is invaluable.

Information is also drawn from the DfEE's good practice guide *Supporting Pupils with Medical Needs* (1996) which should be available in all schools.

This book is unable to cover all the conditions and syndromes that a teacher might meet during a lifetime's teaching. Indeed the medical reference book that does is inches thick. However support groups do exist even for the most unusual and rare conditions. LEAs are now required to keep such a list of those in its area. A number of national groups are listed in the back of this book. Readers who require more help and information about particular conditions should get in touch with the specific voluntary body.

This book adopts a whole school approach to the education of children with serious medical conditions. It is assumed that the school will want the child to be fully integrated into all aspects of school life - 'functional integration' as envisaged by Mary Warnock (1979). It recognises, however, that functional integration presents some challenges that will need to be overcome. It works on the premise that 'forewarned is forearmed' and that knowledge dispels fear.

Part 1 – Developing policies for supporting pupils with medical needs

Chapter 2 of the DfEE's good practice guide *Supporting Pupils with Medical Needs* (1996), suggests that schools should develop a clear policy for supporting children with medical needs which is understood and accepted by staff, parents and pupils. The existence of such a policy could be included in the school's prospectus and be available to parents.

The policy might include the following: (page 6)

- the school's policy on assisting pupils with long-term or complex medical needs

- the need for prior written agreement from parents or guardians for any medication, prescribed, or non-prescription, to be given to the child

- policy on pupils carrying and taking their medication themselves

- staff training in dealing with medical needs

- record keeping

- storage and access to medication

- the school's emergency procedures

Individual schools will want to develop their own policies according to their own needs. As with any school policy one on supporting children with medical needs should be discussed and negotiated with school staff, governors and parents.

Preparation and planning

When a child with a serious medical condition is to be admitted into a mainstream school the teacher and school staff naturally can feel anxious. It is important that information and concerns are shared so that the school staff feel confident and children are prepared. The most important source of information will be the child's parents/carers. They are likely to have experience of living with the condition for some time and will have considerable knowledge and experience to impart to the school. A meeting should be arranged between parents/carers, school and medical staff where issues to do with the child's condition can be frankly discussed. In some cases, particularly for older children, it may be appropriate for the child to be present also. It is important to remember however that all children are individuals, that schools are educational establishments, and that an over-emphasis on the child's condition could be to the detriment of their full integration into school life.

Inevitably, there will be some manifestations of serious medical conditions which require all staff who are working with the child to be more than usually observant and vigilant in order to keep the child well and safe. It is therefore important to have the necessary information. Staff Inset, either by parents or medical staff, might be arranged to prepare all staff and to decide if it is necessary to inform the other children and how this might best be done. Where appropriate it is important to discuss with the child how they would like information about their medical condition communicated to others. Often the child knows a lot about the management of the condition, and if sufficiently mature, should be involved in decisions which affect his/her school experience.

Drawing up a health care plan

The DfEE's good practice guide *Supporting Pupils with Medical Needs* (1996) suggests that an individual health care plan should be set up for pupils with medical needs. This will identify the level of support that is needed by the pupil in school, and the help that the school can provide and should receive. The plan should be a written agreement with the parents which should be reviewed at least annually. For a child with a statement of special educational needs this could form part of the annual review of the statement process. Other children with medical needs may be being monitored through the school-based stages which are subject to regular review. For those children for whom this level of monitoring is not necessary, the review of the individual health care plan provides an opportunity to discuss concerns in a more formal way, although it is highly likely that school and parents will be in regular communication as a matter of policy.

The guide produces a series of example proformas covering such aspects as Request for School to Administer Medication; Request for Child to Carry own Medication; Record of Medication Administered in School; and a health care plan (form 1) as reproduced below.

Health Care Plan for a Pupil with Medical Needs

Name _____

Date of Birth _____

Condition _____

_____

_____

Class/Form _____

_____

_____

Name of School _____

PHOTO

Date _____

Review date _____

CONTACT INFORMATION

Family contact 1

Name _____

Phone No. (work) _____

(home) _____

Relationship _____

Family contact 2

Name _____

Phone No. (work) _____

(home) _____

Relationship _____

Clinic/Hospital contact

Name _____

Phone No. _____

G.P.

Name _____

Phone No. _____

Describe condition and give details of pupil's individual symptoms:

_____

_____

_____

_____

Daily care requirements: (e.g. before sport/at lunchtime)

_____
_____
_____
_____
_____

Describe what constitutes an emergency for the pupil, and the action to take if this occurs:

_____
_____
_____
_____
_____

Follow up care:

_____
_____
_____
_____

Who is responsible in an Emergency: (State if different on off-site activities)

_____
_____
_____
_____
_____

Form copied to:

_____
_____
_____
_____
_____

Reproduced with the DfEE's kind permission from DfEE's good practice guide Supporting Pupils with Medical Needs.

Those who may need to contribute to the healthcare plan are:

- the headteacher

- the parent(s)/carers

- the child (if appropriate)

- classteacher/form tutor/head of year

- care assistant or support staff (if applicable)

- school staff who have agreed to administer medication or be trained in emergency procedures

- the school health service, the child's GP or other health care professionals

It is suggested that a member of staff is given specific responsibility for co-ordinating and disseminating information about the medical needs of individual pupils. The special needs co-ordinator sometimes takes on this role particularly in a secondary school.

Administering medication in school

There is no legal duty which requires school staff to administer medication; this is a voluntary role. Teacher's conditions of employment do not include the giving of medication or supervising a pupil taking it, although staff may volunteer to do this and many are happy to do so (DfEE, 1996 section 28). Any member of staff who agrees to accept responsibility for administering medication will require appropriate training and guidance. The type of training needed will depend upon the individual case and may well arise from the planning consultation with parents when the healthcare plan is being drawn up. NHS Trusts, through the School Health Service, may provide advice and training for school staff in providing for a pupil's medical needs. Most schools will have contact with the health service through a school nurse or doctor.

(Information from: *Supporting Pupils with Medical Needs - A Good Practice Guide.* A joint Dept of Health/DfEE publication)

Part 2 – The education of sick children who are not in school

Children with serious medical conditions often face disruption to their education by periods of ill-health where they are unable to attend school. For some this may mean frequent or extended periods in hospital or at home.

From September 1994, LEAs have had a duty to provide education 'otherwise than at school' where it is necessary to do so to meet the pupil's needs. The DfEE's *Circular 12/94* (part of the *Pupils with Problems* pack which should be available in all schools) sets out those duties and also indicates the responsibilities of schools to maintain contact with the child and to co-operate with the alternative educational provision that may be put in place. Depending on local conditions this may range from education in a hospital school to a few hours of home tuition.

Education in a hospital school (Circular 12/94 sections 4 - 11)

Hospital schools are special schools maintained by the local education authority within the premises of a hospital. Some are in general or district hospitals; others are located within hospitals which provide specialist treatment for children, some of whom will have chronic illnesses.

Education law reflects the special nature and variable circumstances of hospital schools by providing, in some area of legislation, more flexible arrangements than those applying to other special schools. Hospital schools do not have the same legal obligation to provide the National Curriculum as in other special schools, although it is hoped that this will be offered where possible.

Education of children 'otherwise than in school'

Under the *Education Act*, 1993 each local education authority has a duty to make arrangements for the provision of suitable full-time or part-time education at school or otherwise than at school for children of compulsory school age who are unable to attend school by reason of illness.

Education in hospital which is provided as 'education otherwise' by definition means education in hospital *otherwise than a hospital school*.

A hospital unit may be part of a home/hospital teaching service but does not have the legal status of a special school. In practice the provision offered will not be sustantially different and the National Curriculum, while desirable, is not compulsory.

12

Educational provision (Circular 12/94 sections 17 - 47)

The aims of education for children in hospital or receiving home tuition are the same as for all children. The primary aim for hospital/home tuition is to minimise, as far as possible, the interruption and disruption to a child's schooling by continuing education as normally as the child's condition will allow. There should be an emphasis, where possible, on securing the child's return to normal schooling. This applies equally to children with life-threatening conditions and to dying children who have a right to education suited to their age and ability, taking into account their needs and health at the time.

For children who are at home for medical reasons but face only short, infrequent absences from school, for example those lasting less than four weeks, home schools are generally expected to provide work to be done at home where the child's condition allows. Depending on local circumstances and on individual needs, good practice would suggest that children should not be away from school for medical reasons for longer than four weeks without some form of home tuition being arranged. For a child who has previously been in hospital, home tuition may be made available immediately upon discharge.

It is part of the role of the teacher to re-establish learning and to keep education alive in the child's life if disruption is to be minimised. Therefore close liaison between hospital teachers/home tutors/mainstream teachers underpins the provision of an effective educational programme for the child. It is suggested that:

- Hospital teachers/home tutors need a named contact in the child's mainstream or 'home' school in order to exchange information about the pupil. This might be the SEN Co-ordinator, year head or, in a primary school, the headteacher.

- Visits by hospital/home tutors to the child's home school are desirable where practicable.

- Visits to the child in hospital or at home by staff from the home school are not only beneficial educationally but also assist in maintaining the child's morale and self-esteem. Visits or letters from classmates are similarly effective.

- Although not compulsory, in the interest of structure and continuity, hospital teachers generally seek to provide access to the National Curriculum.

- An undue concentration on core subjects and routine work should be avoided when possible.

- When pupils return to school it may be helpful for headteachers to exempt them from the full range of National Curriculum subjects in order that they may readjust.

- Generally, hospitals teach all pupils irrespective of their length of stay.

- Educational provision should commence as soon as is practicable after the child is admitted.

- For long stay pupils (i.e. longer than five working days) planning of education should start straight away, or when practical, before admission.

- Hospital teachers will want to ensure that, even for short-stay patients (i.e. less than five working days), the time spent in hospital is not wasted educationally.

- For pupils undertaking GCSEs in hospital, a concentration on the course work element may help them to keep up with their peers in mainstream schools.

- Liaison between home school and hospital teachers is especially important where the child is moving between home school and the hospital on a regular basis.

- Hospital teachers should keep records of the academic progress of pupils while they are in hospital. Such information should be exchanged with the mainstream school. Agreed proformas may help. A Record of Achievement will give the pupil an opportunity to comment on his/her experiences in hospital. Such comments should be valued by the mainstream school.

- Long-stay pupils may make significant achievements and progress while in hospital. These achievements should not be underestimated, and should be recognised and celebrated by the pupil's mainstream school.

- Short-stay pupils should be encouraged to take back to their home school any school-work they have done in hospital.

(Summarised from *Circular 12/94* sections 17 - 47)

14

Pupils taught 'otherwise than in school' and who have special educational needs

Most pupils being taught in hospital or receiving home tuition are from mainstream schools. They do not necessarily have learning difficulties as outlined in the *Code of Practice* (1994) and their abilities and attainments are likely to span the whole ability range. However, some long-stay pupils in hospital schools may require a statutory assessment and the drawing up of a statement if their condition requires it, or if their special educational needs are to be met in the hospital school for the foreseeable future. Statutory assessment or re-assessment may need to be undertaken if the pupil's needs change significantly or there is a deterioration in the child's condition.

(Information from: *Circular 12/94 The Education of Sick Children.* A joint DfEE/Dept of Health Circular)

Part 3 – The Code of Practice and medical conditions

In the *Education Act* 1993 the then government promised to publish a *Code of Practice* for the education of children with special educational needs. The terms 'learning difficulty' and 'special educational needs' were defined.

A child has special educational needs if s/he has a learning difficulty which calls for special educational provision to be made for him/her.

Pupils with special *medical* needs will not necessarily have special *educational* needs as defined above. For those that do, schools will find the *Code of Practice on the Identification and Assessment of Special Educational Needs* (DfEE, 1994) helpful. The booklet *Spotlight on Special Educational Needs: Learning Difficulties* (Beveridge, 1996) will also be of assistance.

However some children with special medical difficulties will require close and careful monitoring to ensure that they have access to a 'broad and balanced curriculum' as is their entitlement. For example, if the condition results in frequent, unavoidable absences, or drug therapy which severely affects feelings of well-being and motivation, schools may wish to conduct their monitoring under the school-based stages of assessment (Stages 1-3) as outlined in the Code (para 2:61). For most children with serious medical conditions all five stages will not be necessary.

15

At Stage 1 a child's teacher will identify and register the special educational/medical needs, consult the parent(s)/carers and take initial action. The Stage 1 action plan should be reviewed 'within a term.' Many children with special medical needs may remain at Stage 1 for some time or indeed throughout their education. The advantage of being placed on the special needs register means that the child's needs are regularly reviewed and parents consulted. Any concerns can be aired and appropriate action taken.

At Stages 2 and 3 an IEP (Individual Education Plan) will be drawn up and targets set and monitored. At Stage 3 schools may wish to enlist the help of outside agencies, such as advisory support staff, educational welfare staff and/or educational psychologists. The advice of medical and para-medical staff (physiotherapists, occupational therapists and speech therapists) may well be needed in some cases and at any stage. Depending on local circumstances, outreach support from local special or hospital schools may be available.

The setting up of a health care plan, the annual review of that plan as outlined in Part Two, the monitoring of special needs through the school-based stages of assessment, and close and regular contact with parent(s)/carers mean that for the vast majority of children with serious medical conditions their needs can be met by their mainstream school without the need to arrange special educational provision by way of a statutory assessment and a statement of special educational needs.

However the Code makes it clear that for a small number of children the medical condition may have a significant impact on the child's academic progress and/or access to the curriculum in its broadest sense. In these cases schools may wish to request that the local education authority considers making a statutory assessment of the child's needs with a view to issuing a statement of special educational needs.

Paragraphs 3:89 - 3:94 of the *Code of Practice* (1994) clearly set out the criteria by which the LEA should consider such a request for children with serious medical conditions and are set out below for ease of reference (pp 67 - 69).

Criteria for statutory assessment of children with medical conditions
'3:89 Some medical conditions, if appropriate action is not taken, may have a significant impact on the child's academic attainment and/or may give rise to emotional and behavioural difficulties. Some of the commonest medical difficulties are likely to be congenital heart disease, epilepsy, asthma, cystic fibrosis, haemophilia, sickle cell anaemia, diabetes, renal failure, eczema, rheumatoid disorders, and leukaemia and childhood cancers.'

16

'3:90 These conditions may in themselves significantly impair the child's ability to participate fully in the curriculum and the wider range of activities in the school. Some medical conditions may affect the child's progress and performance intermittently, others on a continuous basis throughout the child's school career. Drug therapies, such as those required for the treatment of leukaemia and childhood cancers, may compound the problems of the condition and have implications for the child's education. The medication required for the control of epilepsy may similarly impair concentration and cause difficulties in the classroom. In some instances, children and young people with potentially life-threatening conditions such as cystic fibrosis or heart disease may have periods of hospitalisation and emotional and behavioural difficulties related to their conditions and associated restrictions on everyday living and the nature of the treatment required.'

'3:91 Consultation and open discussion with the child's parents, the school, the school doctor or the child's general practitioner, the community paediatrician and any specialist services providing treatment for the child will be essential to ensure that the child achieves maximum progress and also that the child is not unnecessarily excluded from any part of the curriculum or school activity because of anxiety about his or her care and treatment.'

The child's learning difficulty

'3:92 The LEA should seek clear recorded evidence of both the child's academic attainment and the nature of his or her medical condition, asking, for example, whether:

i. there is a significant discrepancy between the child's attainment, as measured by National Curriculum assessments and tests, and teacher's own recorded assessments of a child's classroom work, including any portfolio of the child's work, and the attainment of the majority of children of his or her age

ii. there is a significant discrepancy between the expectations of the child as assessed by the child's teachers, parents and external specialists who have closely observed the child, supported as appropriate by the results of standardised tests of cognitive ability, and the child's attainment as measured by National Curriculum assessments and tests

iii. there is clear recorded evidence that the child's medical condition significantly impedes or disrupts his or her access to the curriculum, ability to take part in particular classroom activities or participation in aspects of school life

iv. *there is clear substantiated evidence, based on specific examples,*
   that the child's medical condition has given rise to emotional and
   behavioural difficulties
v. *there is evidence of significant and recurrent absences from school'*

The child's special educational provision
   '3:93 In the light of evidence about the child's academic attainment and
medical condition, the LEA should consider the action taken by the school
and, in particular, should ask whether:
   i. *the school has, with the parents' consent, notified and sought the*
      assistance of the school doctor, the child's general pratitioner or any
      specialist child health service, as appropriate
   ii. *all staff have been fully informed of the child's medical condition*
      and a consistent approach to managing the child's education has
      been taken across the school
   iii. *the school has sought the views of and involved the parents at each stage*
   iv. *the school has sought the co-operation of those within the local*
      authority responsible for the education of children who are at home
      and, as appropriate, in hospital, as a result of illness

3:94 Where the balance of evidence presented to and assessed by the
LEA suggests that the child's learning difficulties and/or disabilities:

• *are significant and/or complex*

• *have not been met by relevant or purposeful measures taken by the*
  school and external specialists

• *may call for special educational provision which cannot reasonably be*
  provided within the rosources normally available to mainstream
  schools in the area the LEA should consider very carefully the case for
  a statutory assessment of the child's special educational needs.'
                                     (*Code of Practice, 1994* pp 67 - 69)

Part 4 – Medical conditions

This chapter outlines eight of the more common serious medical
conditions which may be found in mainstream classrooms. Each
description is followed by notes on the treatment of the condition and the
educational/care implications for school staff.

Information has been drawn from publications produced by relevant voluntary organisations and either adapted or reproduced here with their permission. In each case the voluntary organisation was consulted with regards to accuracy of information but readers are urged to contact them directly for more detailed help and advice. A list of organisations appears at the end of this book.

Diabetes

One in 700 children of school age has diabetes. It is therefore likely that, at some time, school staff will teach or supervise a child with the condition. Therefore staff working with a child with diabetes should be aware of the causes, treatment, management and possible medical needs of the condition in order to know how to help keep the child healthy and safe.

It is important to plan for the entry into school of a child with diabetes, to inform school staff and to discuss with the child and the parents about how best to inform the rest of the class.

Description

Diabetes, or to give it its proper name, *diabetes mellitus*, is a condition in which the amount of glucose (sugar) in the blood is too high because the body is unable to use it properly. This is because the body's method of converting glucose into energy is not working as it should.

Normally the amount of glucose in our blood is carefully controlled by the hormone insulin. Insulin is made by a gland called the pancreas which lies just behind the stomach. Insulin helps the glucose to enter the cells where it is used as fuel by the body.

We obtain glucose from the food we eat, either from sweet foods or from the digestion of starchy foods such as bread, pasta, cereals and rice.

After a meal including those starchy foods, the blood glucose level rises and insulin is released into the blood. When the blood glucose level falls (for example during exercise), the level of insulin falls. Insulin, therefore, plays a vital role in regulating the level of blood glucose, and, in particular, in stopping the blood glucose from rising too high.

Children with diabetes have lost the ability to produce insulin because the cells in the pancreas that produce it have been destroyed. Without insulin, the child's body cannot use glucose and therefore the blood glucose level will rise. When this happens, the excess glucose will leak into the urine causing frequent passing of urine and increased thirst. Because the body cannot use glucose, fat is broken down instead, leading

19

to weight loss. Therefore, a child with *undiagnosed* and *untreated* diabetes will show symptoms of thirst, frequent trips to the toilet, weight loss and tiredness.

Treatment

Diabetes cannot be cured, but it can be treated effectively. Children with diabetes need to:

have daily insulin injections
eat regular, appropriate food
and
monitor their blood glucose level

On the whole children with diabetes are very good at managing their own condition and recognising when things are not right.

The aim of the treatment is to keep the blood glucose level close to the normal range so that the blood glucose is neither too high (**hyper**glycaemia) nor too low (**hypo**glycaemia).

Insulin Injections

Children with diabetes need to balance their insulin with the food they eat and their level of physical activity. The majority of school age children with diabetes require two insulin injections a day. Most children do their own injections from an early age and it is unlikely that these will need to be given at school. In the unlikely situation of a child needing to inject at school they may need supervision if very young and/or a suitable, private place to carry out the procedure.

Regular appropriate food

Children with diabetes do not require a 'special diet'. The food recommended for children with diabetes is based on that recommended for all children i.e. a healthy, varied diet. Food choices should be generally low in sugar and fat and high in fibre. Meals should be based on starchy foods. The child with diabetes will know how to pay particular attention to carbohydrate foods, such as bread, pasta, rice, potatoes and cereals.

However children with diabetes must be allowed to eat regularly during the day. The timing of mealtimes is important and may include eating snacks during classtime.

Timing of mealtimes and snacks

Because the child needs to eat on time s/he may need to be near the front of the queue and/or at the same sitting each day for the midday meal. Most children with diabetes will also need snacks between meals. These could be cereal bars, fruit, crisps or biscuits. The snacks may occasionally need to be eaten during class time. Staff in charge of sports or other activity sessions should be aware that excessive exercise can cause a hypoglycaemic reaction and should ensure that glucose tablets, a sugary snack or drink is taken beforehand and that some glucose is to hand should it be needed.

Monitoring blood glucose level

A regular check needs to be kept to ensure that blood glucose levels remain stable. Most children will do this themselves. It is done by a simple finger prick blood test. The test takes about two minutes and can be done in the classroom, on the school bus or any convenient place. The child will have his/her own container for disposing of blood testing equipment.

The treatment of insulin injections and regular meals is carried out in order to maintain blood glucose at a near normal level - if the blood glucose level should drop a hypoglycaemic reaction (a 'hypo') may result.

Most hypos can be identified and treated without calling for specialist medical help. **It is important, however to know what causes hypoglycaemia, how to recognise it and what action to take.**

The common **causes** of hypoglycaemia are:

a missed or delayed meal
extra exercise (above that anticipated)
too much insulin

Hypoglycaemia may occur more frequently when it is either very hot or very cold.

The **symptoms** of hypoglycaemia in a child with diabetes vary from child to child but can include:

• hunger

• sweating

• drowsiness

• pallor

21

- glazed eyes

- shaking

- mood changes

- lack of concentration

- irritability

Many children with diabetes recognise the on-coming symptoms themselves and will communicate this to an adult and ask for a snack or a sweet or drink.

The **treatment** of hypoglycaemia in a child with diabetes is: **Give a fast acting sugar immediately**. Examples of fast acting sugars are:

- sugary drinks (Lucozade, Fanta, Coke, not diet varieties)

- mini chocolate bars

- glucose tablets

- honey or jam or 'Hypo-stop' - a glucose gel which parents can provide.

If the child is unable to swallow, try rubbing jam, honey or 'hypo-stop' inside the cheek where it can be absorbed.

Do not send a child who is hypo to get sugary food - always send someone else or make sure they are accompanied.

In the unlikely event of the child losing consciousness, place in the recovery position and call an ambulance. The child will come round eventually with the correct treatment and should not come to any immediate harm.

The British Diabetic Association (address at the end of this book) publishes a series of five school cards which cover such items as:

- planning for the child with diabetes

- food

- physical activity

- trips away from home

- and a diabetes record card which should be filled in with the parents.

Educational implications
Teachers and other school staff need to be aware of the care implications
as outlined above otherwise the education of children with diabetes should
be the same as for any other child according to their age and abilities. They
should have full access to the broad and balanced curriculum, including the
National Curriculum, that is the entitlement of all children and should have
access to the full range of activities such as sports/drama and school trips.
Unless there are other special educational needs it is unlikely that a child
with diabetes will need a statutory assessment and a statement of special
educational needs.

(Information provided by British Diabetic Association in *Children with
Diabetes -guidance for teachers and school staff*)

Epilepsy
Approximately one in 200 of the population are affected with
epilepsy. The majority of people with epilepsy have their first seizure
before the age of 20. It is highly likely therefore that most teachers will
have several children with epilepsy in their classes at some time during
their careers.

Description
Epilepsy is an 'established tendency to recurrent seizures'. Even
though seizures look different and affect children in different ways,
they are caused by the same thing - a brief malfunction in the brain's
biochemistry.

Epilepsy is not a disease or illness, but it may be a symptom of some
physical disorder. However in many cases there may be no identifiable
cause.

Seizures may produce changes in consciousness and perception,
involuntary movements, muscle spasms, and sometimes convulsions. They
may be over in seconds or last a few minutes.

We used to know epilepsy as either 'grand mal' or 'petit mal'. It is now
recognised that there are a number of different types of seizures from the
'tonic-clonic' or convulsive seizure through 'absences' to sub-clinical
seizures. (International League against Epilepsy (1982) *International
Classification of Seizures*)

23

HOW TO RECOGNISE A SEIZURE AND WHAT TO DO

	NAME OF SEIZURE	WHAT IT LOOKS LIKE	BE ALERT FOR	WHAT YOU CAN DO
GENERALISED SEIZURE (Affects the whole brain)	ABSENCE (previously called petit mal)	Most common in children who may look blank, stare and may have slight twitching or blinking. Lasts a few seconds.	Person may be unaware of seizure. It may be mistaken for daydreaming.	Be understanding. Repeat what has been missed. Note that it has happened.
	TONIC CLONIC (previously called grand mal)	The body will stiffen and may involve a cry (this is not pain), followed by a fall; convulsions then begin and the child may go blue due to a lack of oxygen. Incontinence may occur. Lasts a few minutes.	An aura of warning known to that person. Fatigue or headache.	Protect from injury. Cushion the head. Help breathing by turning the person on their side. Stay with the person until fully recovered. Do not restrict movements or put anything into the mouth or give a drink.
PARTIAL SEIZURE (Affects part of the brain)	COMPLEX PARTIAL	May start with an "aura" or warning - visual, auditory, taste etc. The person may appear conscious but may not respond. Abnormal movements like plucking at clothing, smacking of lips may occur. They may want to wander about aimlessly. They usually last ½ to 2 minutes or so.	Irrational behaviour and confusion. May be misunderstood for behavioural problems.	Do not try to stop the seizure. Guide from danger if possible. Be understanding and talk reassuringly.

Reproduced with kind permission of British Epilepsy Association.

Treatment

The management of epileptic seizures is outlined below in 'Educational Implications'. However, many teachers in mainstream classes rarely, if ever, see a seizure despite having a child with epilepsy in the class. Fortunately, anti-epileptic medication controls the seizures and gives most children the chance to lead normal lives. It is important to remember that eight out of ten children with epilepsy lead trouble free, enjoyable lives.

For those very few children with intractible, uncontrolled epilepsy it will take some time to find the correct type and dose of medication. Sometimes these children are monitored in a hospital or special school setting. Treatment in these instances will consist of medication, management of the seizures, careful recording of the frequency and duration of the seizures and a great deal of sympathetic understanding.

Educational implications

Epilepsy can affect people of all ages, backgrounds and levels of intelligence. Therefore children who have seizures should have the same educational opportunities as others and a chance to learn in a normal educational setting.

Teachers should be aware that many children with epilepsy perform below their capabilities. This may be because the medication is causing the child to be drowsy, or over-active, and needs adjusting. In some cases the child may experience a loss of self-esteem if the seizures are not well handled and understood by adults and children in his or her life.

Teachers and other school staff have a vital role to play not only in the academic life of a child with epilepsy but also in their physical and emotional well-being. Communication between teacher, parents/carers, doctors and pupil is of vital importance.

Absence seizures (previously petit mal epilepsy) may pass unnoticed. Frequently there is only a brief, staring spell or fluttering of the eyelids. The child is unaware that it has happened. A calm, matter-of-fact approach and understanding by the teacher are all that are needed. If absences occur frequently the child may experience some learning difficulties and find it hard to keep up with their peers. Therefore it is often important to record the frequency of the absences.

Tonic-clonic seizures (previously grand mal epilepsy) may last several minutes and may be alarming to teachers and other pupils at first. The teacher needs to feel confident in the care and after care of the child if a seizure occurs. Seek advice from parents and medical staff. If possible establish the procedure to be followed long before a seizure occurs. It would be particularly helpful for a teacher who has a child with epilepsy in the class to have accesss to another adult. A routine for calling for assistance should be established.

It is important to observe the following rules:

- Stay calm

- Reassure the other children

- Only move the child if there is danger of them hurting themselves.

LET THE SEIZURE RUN ITS COURSE
1. Cushion the head with something soft but do not try to restrain convulsive movements.
2. Do not try to put anything at all beween the teeth.
3. Do not give anything to drink.
4. Gently loosen tight clothing around the neck.
5. Do not call for an ambulance unless you suspect *status epilepticus* (see later).
6. As soon as the convulsions have stopped turn the child into the recovery position. Wipe away saliva from the mouth.
7. If incontinence occurs cover the child to prevent embarrassment.
8. If the child is confused following the seizure be calm and reassuring. Allow the child to rest if necessary.

It is often helpful to record the type and length of the seizure and to inform parents via a note or phone call at the end of the day. It is not necessary except in extreme cases to send the child home after a seizure.

NB. Some people with epilepsy do experience seizures which last for as long as five minutes or even longer on a regular basis and recover normally. However this is *not the norm* and teachers and other school staff should be aware of anyone in their class who experiences seizures of this length.

Status Epilepticus is one of the rare medical emergencies associated with epilepsy which requires immediate treatment.

1. If a child has a seizure which shows no sign of stopping after four minutes, or
2. a series of seizures takes place without the child properly regaining consciousness in between.

In this case call a doctor or an ambulance. Inform the parents as soon as possible.

(Information provided by British Epilepsy Society in *Epilepsy - A guide for teachers* and National Society for Epilepsy - *Epilepsy at School*)

Epilepsy and special educational needs

Children with epilepsy do not have learning difficulties as part of the condition. With correct medication they can remain free of seizures and reach their academic potential. With adequate, but not over-protective, supervision they should have access to the whole currriculum including swimming and other forms of sport, and laboratory work. For a very small minority, the condition can be so disabling as to interfere with normal life at home and at school. These children may require a statutory assessment as outlined in the *Code of Practice* (1994) and may need a statement of special educational needs and require specialist provision.

FIRST AID FOR SEIZURES ...

Better education and a more open attitude to epilepsy and first aid should help everyone to feel confident and calm when helping a person who is having a seizure.

No first aid is required for many types of seizures. The main exceptions are tonic-clonic and complex partial seizures. These are described in the chart on page 24.

Seizures can be allowed to run their natural course following these guidelines. Recovery times may vary from person to person. Some people need to rest for a few seconds, while others need to sleep for varying periods.

DO cushion the head with hands/forearms if nothing else available.
DO turn them over into the above position once it is over - it will help them breathe.
DO NOT move them during the seizure unless there is danger.
DO NOT put anything between the teeth.
DO NOT restrict their movement.

Reproduced with kind permission of British Epilepsy Association.

Cystic Fibrosis

Cystic fibrosis is the most common life-threatening inherited disorder among Caucasian people in the UK. It affects about one in 2,500 live births.

Description

In a child with cystic fibrosis the body produces a thick, sticky mucous affecting several organs but particularly the lungs and digestive system. Mucous in the lungs attracts infection and children often have a persistent (non infective) cough and asthmatic wheezing. The inflammation associated with persistent chest infections progressively damages the lungs. Damage to the pancreas means that the production of digestive enzymes is severely impaired and necessitates the taking of enzyme capsules with all meals and snacks to aid absorption of food. Other effects of CF may be sinusitis, hay fever, arthritis or diabetes. Rarer complications, usually appearing in older children and adults, include heart strain and liver damage. CF affects individual children in different ways and in varying degrees of severity. Their needs can change from month to month and even from day to day. It is important to maintain close contact with medical advisers and the family and heed their advice.

For most childen in school effective treatment consists of daily physiotherapy, high calorie diet and antibiotics, which will require a level of support and supervision especially in younger children.

The future prognosis for each child with CF is unsure, but most children now live into adulthood and learn to manage their disability. The outlook has improved significantly in recent years owing to the improvements in effective treatments, dietary care and powerful medication. In some severe cases successful lung transplants have been carried out. The gene that causes CF has been isolated and laboratory and clinical studies have started to determine the possibility of 'gene therapy' - replacing the faulty gene with a healthy one.

Educational implications

- As with other serious medical conditions a health care plan should be drawn up which involves parents, pupil (if appropriate), school and medical staff (see part 2). Decisions with regard to the carrying out of treatment and the supervision of medication may need to be made.

- The presence of the condition itself is not significant educationally and children with cystic fibrosis will be as academically able as their peers and should have access to the whole range of the curriculum as is their entitlement (but see CF and special educational needs).

28

- Physiotherapy treatments need to be carried out two or three times a day. It is therefore very likely that treatment will need to be carried out during the school day. The techniques of breathing control and postural drainage are relatively easy to learn and can be carried out by a care or special support assistant.

- The number of physiotherapy sessions that need to be carried out in a day varies depending on the child's current state of health. More sessions may need to be built into the day following a cold or chest infection. Parents and/or the child will be able to advise.

- Physiotherapy needs to be carried out before meals. This will require a level of planning and understanding from the child's teachers. Medication needs to be taken with meals.

- Most children with CF become independent from an early age - certainly by adolesence - and require a minimum of support.

- Physiotherapy may be combined with nebuliser treatment (see part 5 - asthma).

Antibiotics may be taken orally, via the nebuliser or in some cases administered intravenously.

- Some supervision of medication: pancreatin, antibiotics, vitamins etc will be required particularly with younger children (see part 1 on the responsibilities of teachers in the administration of drugs).

- Full participation in the curriculum should also include access to PE and games and outside play when the child is well. Physical exercise is known to be beneficial. However if the child is suffering from a cold or recently returned following a chest infection s/he may be tired and lacking in energy. Teachers may find it necessary to make alternative arrangements for a short while until the child is fully recovered.

Cystic fibrosis and special educational needs
If treament is carried out with minimum disruption to their day-to-day school lives children with cystic fibrosis do not normally have learning difficulties.
However a child with CF may have special educational needs if the condition results in the child having significant periods of absence from school and

for example 'prevents or hinders the child from making use of the educational facilities of a kind provided for children of the same age within the area of the local educational authority'(*Code of Practice 1994*). There will be occasions, particularly in the winter months when the child with CF is feeling unwell because of, or following a cold or chest infection. Opportunities should be given to allow the child to 'catch up' with work missed.

Frequent absences and/or hospitalisations resulting in the child missing large elements of the curriculum can be minimised by close co-operation of teachers, parents and home or hospital tutors. School may wish to monitor progress through the school-based stages of assessment.

As with all serious medical conditions, teachers should be aware of the psychological pressures on parents of children with CF. It is a chronic, life-threatening condition and the pressures on the child and the whole family can be considerable. There is also a genetic element and more than one child in the family can be affected. This can lead to uncertainty about the child's future, worry and tiredness from coping with the demanding routine of supervising medication and physiotherapy.

Some serious psychological problems may occur in adolesence when the young person realises the seriousness of the condition. At this time sympathetic understanding and probably counselling are required.

(Information provided by Cystic Fibrosis Trust in *Cystic Fibrosis and School*)

Asthma

Asthma is a growing problem amongst school children. About one in ten children of primary school age has asthma, although the severity of the condition varies from child to child. Some children just have an occasional cough, wheeze, tight chest or shortness of breath and need their reliever inhaler when these symptoms appear. Others need regular preventer and reliever medication and may miss periods of school; for a tiny minority the condition is life-threatening.

Description

Asthma is a condition in which the air passages in the lungs become narrowed making it difficult to breath. Sudden narrowing produces an 'asthma attack'.

People with asthma have airways which are almost continuously inflamed. Inflamed airways are quick to react to certain triggers (irritants) that do not affect other children who do not have asthma.

Common triggers include:

- viral infections

- allergies, like pet fur for example

- dust mites

- vigorous exercise

- sudden changes in temperature, strong winds

- excitement or prolonged laughing

- fumes, such as glue, paint and tobacco smoke

Treatment
1. Relievers or bronchodilators: an inhaler which is designed to give immediate relief by opening up the airways when the symptoms of an asthma attack appear.
2. Preventative treatment: inhalers that are taken regularly to damp down the sensitivity of the air passages so that attacks no longer occur or are only mild.
3. For a small minority of children with asthma a nebuliser may be needed. This is an electronically powered device used to deliver their asthma medication.

Educational implications
Educational implications for children with asthma are largely concerned with an understanding of the condition by teachers, other school staff and classmates, the need for access to reliever medication and what to do in the event of an attack.

Advice from parents and medical practitioners should be sought before the child enters the school/class and a health care plan drawn up (see part 1).

Access to medication: **Children with asthma must have immediate access to their reliever inhalers when they need them.**

- Decisions with regard to where the inhaler is kept must remain a matter of the professional judgement of the headteacher in consultation with the parents and medical practitioners. Schools should develop a consistent policy which is known, understood and followed by all staff who come into contact with the child and by the child and classmates.

- Most children with asthma learn quickly how to use their inhalers properly and it is good practice to allow them to keep their inhalers with them at all times.

- If the child is too young, or not considered reliable enough by parent/teacher, to do this, and school take responsibility for the safe-keeping of inhalers, **access should never be restricted**.

- Inhalers should be labelled with the child's name and its location known and accessible to the child and responsible adults at all times of the school day.

- It is recommended that the reliever inhaler is kept in the classroom near the child and taken to other parts of the school with the child when s/he is not in the classroom.

- It is important to ensure that a child does not have to walk long distances e.g. off playing fields, nor climb stairs to get to their inhaler when they are breathless. Another child or adult could be sent while the teacher stays with the child.

- It is a good idea to ask parents to supply a spare inhaler so that one is always available in case of loss or damage.

- Nebulisers and other drugs should be stored by the school.

- Children with asthma on school trips, whatever their duration, should have access to their inhalers at all times.

How to help during an asthma attack

- ensure that reliever inhaler is taken straight away

- stay calm and reassure the child - it is comforting to have a hand to hold

- talk quietly to them

- loosen tight clothing around the neck

- encourage the child to breath slowly and deeply

- allow the child to sit in a comfortable position - do not let them lie down

- after an attack encourage the child to return to normal activities as soon as possible

Call a doctor or ambulance if:

- the reliever inhaler has no effect after 5-10 minutes

- the child becomes distressed or is unable to talk

- the child is becoming exhausted

- you have any doubts about the child's condition

If you are worried, do not be afraid of causing a fuss.

Asthma and exercise
'Total normal activity' should be the goal for all but those with severe asthma.

- It is important that childen with asthma are encouraged to take part in all school activities including sport

- reliever medication should be taken beforehand and kept with the child during the PE lesson. Some medication (e.g. Intal) needs to be taken half an hour before exercise

- children should 'warm up' before playing games

- if children with asthma become wheezy during exercise let them take their reliever inhaler if they need it

- for children with 'exercise induced' asthma the type of sport and weather conditions are often critical. Cold, dry air can trigger asthma in some children and cross country running can be a problem

- swimming is an excellent form of exercise for children with asthma

Children with asthma and special educational needs
Children with asthma do not have learning difficulties as a part of the
condition. As with some other serious medical conditions they may experience
special educational needs as a result of prolonged absences from school or
hospitalisations. Disturbed nights due to asthma symptoms may reduce
concentration levels in the classroom. Schools may wish to monitor educational
progress via the school-based stages of assessment but it is unlikely that a
statement of special needs will be required except in very exceptional
circumstances (see The Code of Practice and medical conditions, part 3).

(Information provided by National Asthma Campaign in *Asthma at
School* and other publications)

ME - Myalgic Encephalomyelitis (also know as post viral fatigue syndrome)
Description
Myalgic encephalomyelitis (ME) means 'inflammation of the central
nervous system and muscles'.

Research increasingly suggests that ME is due to a persistent viral
infection, an overactive immune system, or both. ME is usually triggered
by viral illnesses such as flu or glandular fever, but other triggers reported
have included vaccinations, stress and accidents. For some, ME sets in with
no obvious trigger.

ME has only recently been recognised in children as an organic illness.
Whereas ten years ago, children with ME were rarely diagnosed, a growing
number are now being recognised as suffering from it. Indeed, children
represent around 10 per cent of ME sufferers - giving a figure of 25,000
child cases as a minimum (Colby, 1996).

The symptoms of ME are:

• fatigue, made worse by minimal physical and/or mental exertion

• prolonged recovery period made worse by inappropriate diagnosis
  and/or treatment in the early stages

• impairment of short-term memory and concentration

• fluctuation of symptoms, usually caused by physical or mental activity

Other symptoms particularly noticed in children are: pain in joints and
muscles; severe headaches not generally relieved by pain-killers; twitching
muscles; pins and needles; lack of ability to think straight or talk properly;
hypersensitivity to light, sound and smell; faintness and heart symptoms.

Psychological symptoms such as mood swings and even panic attacks have been noted. ME however is not of psychological origin. It has been shown (Ho-Yen, 1995) that where psychological symptoms do exist, it is as a result of the ME not the cause of it.

The sufferer can vary from sheer exhaustion to near normality quite suddenly. It is difficult to believe that a child who is often physically exhausted can also become hyperactive. 'There's nothing wrong with *him*!' can be a common and natural reaction. Unless there is an understanding of the condition by friends and significant adults in the child's life this may be interpreted as 'malingering' or chronic 'school phobia'. Diagnosis is a matter for the medical profession but there is much that teachers and schools can do to recognise the symptoms of ME, particularly in a previously healthy and well-motivated student, and where necessary to sympathetically address the educational needs of pupils diagnosed as suffering from ME.

Educational implications
- Co-operation between parents, ME sufferer, medical and school staff is vital to manage the illness and to maximise the pupil's ability to access educational provision.

- Some pupils will be well enough to come into school on a full or part-time basis. Others will need a prolonged period at home and a gentle and planned reintegration into school.

The pupil at school or on return to school

- As with other chronic illnesses children with ME are often very knowledgeable about their condition. They should therefore be involved in planning programmes of work as they are aware of how much energy is available on a given day. Rest may be needed after travel or physical or mental activity. Onset of fatigue may include; pallor, remoteness, deteriorating concentration and work quality and output.

- It is counterproductive to push these children beyond their limits - although they will sometimes do this themselves.

- Powers of concentration, comprehension and deduction may be affected.

- Children with ME may not be able to undertake the full range of National Curriculum subjects. Therefore it is necessary, with the student, to prioritise what is to be taught and learnt.

- There must be flexibility of pace. There will be good days, and bad days when exhaustion may suddenly set in. Teachers should be aware of the symptoms of fatigue.

- In particular the student's participation in the PE curiculum needs to be carefully planned - swimming is for example much more gentle than running, and PE may need to be omitted altogether at the early stages of the illness or after a prolonged period off school.

- Prolonged or frequent absences from school may leave the student with gaps in the work covered by the other children. They may be unable to catch up totally when they return and striving to do so may precipitate another relapse.

- In class, teachers need to be aware of the following potential difficulties:
  low tolerance of smells and substances e.g. in the laboratory
  temperature problems
  need for frequent visits to the toilet
  need for frequent food and/or drink
  forgetfulness/lack of concentration
  emotional stress, anxiety and even panic

- Special arrangements for exams may need to be made by giving the student extra time or rests during the exam. Public exam boards will make special concessions provided sufficient time is given.

The pupil with ME at home
- At the beginning of the illness the child needs an adequate period of planned rest/activity probably at home. Fluctuations and relapses are to be expected and the child and parents may become very despondent.

- Pupils at home for any length of time become separated from their peers, lose social contact and can be very isolated. Friends should be encouraged to visit when appropriate and the child should be encouraged to get out of the house when they feel well enough.

- A sympathetic home tutor can not only maintain the pupil's education but can help to keep him/her buoyant.

- Staff at school need to be aware of the social difficulties that some students with ME face. Because of the fluctuating nature of the illness it is not unknown for the student's peers to be disbelieving about the condition and to see it as an excuse for 'skiving' which can be distressing and hurtful. This is particularly common after a period at home and teachers should be aware of unkind teasing or even bullying that can occur. As with other conditions it is important to consult the student as to how much and in what way his/her peers should be informed about the condition.

(Information provided by Action for ME in: *Guidelines for Schools*)

ME and special educational needs

Students with ME do not have learning difficulties as described in the *Code of Practice* (1994), but depending on the severity of the illness and/or the length of absence from school may meet the criteria for statutory assessment and may or may not require a statement of special educational needs. Schools may wish to monitor progress through the school-based stages of assessment and the student's name should be added to the register of special needs. Schools will certainly want to make full use of support services available such as school medical service, education welfare, educational psychologist and home tuition. In some cases, depending on local circumstances, transport to and from school can be arranged.

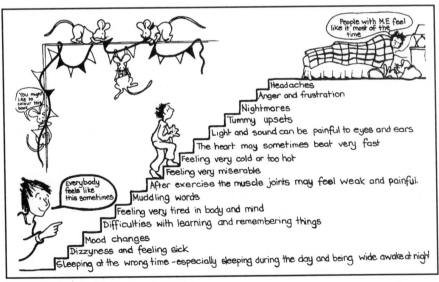

From: 'What is ME', a booklet for children published by Action for ME.

Childhood Cancers

Cancer is comparitively rare in children. There are only 1,300 new cases of childhood cancer in the UK each year, giving an annual incidence rate of one per 10,000 children. Improved survival rates in children with cancer are as a result of considerable advances in treatment over the last three decades. As a result many children with cancer are alive and well after five years and a substantial number make a full recovery.

However the diagnosis, and susequent treatment, will affect the education, psychological well-being and social life of the child, his/her family, teachers and classmates. It is important therefore that there is an understanding of the causes of the disease and the possible side effects of the treatment, by teachers and other school staff, so that the child can be supported through what is a difficult and traumatic time.

What is cancer?

Despite much research, the causes of cancer in children are not well understood. What is known is that cancer occurs when some of the body's cells become abnormal and multiply in an uncontrolled way forming a lump or tumour, such as a brain tumour, or proliferating in the blood system causing leukaemia. What is not known is *why* this happens.

In cancer the lump or tumour is malignant. A malignant tumour has the potential to spread into other tissues or organs via the blood or lymphatic systems. It is this potential to spread that makes cancer a life-threatening disease.

Leukaemia is the commonest form of cancer in children. It results from an uncontrolled production of abnormal blood cells. Swollen glands are formed which are collections of abnormal 'leukaemic' cells. Symptoms are: lack of energy, anaemia, susceptibility to infection, abnormal bleeding and bruising.

Solid tumours may occur in almost any part of the body. The commonest sites in children are: brain tumours, kidneys (Wilm's tumour), lymph nodes (Hodgkin's disease/Non-Hodgkin's lymphoma), nerve cells (neuroblastoma), muscle cells (rhabdomyosarcoma), back of the eye (retinoblastoma) and bone tumours (osteosarcoma and Ewing's sarcoma). Symptoms vary according to the site of the tumour.

Treatment of childhood cancers

There are three main types of cancer treatment which may be used alone or in combination depending upon the tumour and the individual child. They are: chemotherapy, surgery and radiotherapy.

Chemotherapy is treatment by drugs. A combination of drugs, two or three are often used, circulate through the body killing the malignant cells. Leukaemia is usually treated in this way. In solid tumours chemotherapy is sometimes given to reduce the size of the tumour to make its removal by surgery easier. Chemotherapy can also be given after surgical removal.

Surgery is the removal of the tumour and sometimes surrounding tissue by operation. Brain tumours are usually surgically removed.

Radiotherapy is treatment by radiation. Special equipment directs the rays to the tumour for a few minutes which kills the malignant cells. Radiotherapy may be given pre or post operatively, or in combination with chemotherapy.

Side effects of treatment

Probably the most obvious, and for many children the most distressing, side effect of cancer treatment is change in physical appearance, particularly loss of hair. It is important to remember that most physical side effects will reverse once treatment has stopped. Hair will usually regrow, although sometimes differently. Wearing a jaunty hat, wig or pretty scarf can help disguise hair loss until this happens. Other changes in appearance can be obvious weight loss or gain, a puffiness or 'moon-faced' look, and ulcers around the mouth. Altered body image can cause enormous problems to children and young people and should not be minimised. Teachers and classmates need to be prepared in order to welcome the sick child back to school.

Other side effects of treatment can be: nausea; fatigue; drowsiness; aches and pains; difficulties with walking, co-ordination and concentration.

Treatment, remission and relapse

The first phase of cancer treatment is intensive and usually given in hospital. It can be chemotherapy, surgery or radiotherapy or a combination of two or all three.

Remission is the period when the cancer is under control and the child is not showing any signs of the disease. Children usually feel well and return to full time schooling. Only after several years of remission can the child be considered to be cured of the cancer. In some cases a **relapse** may occur. This is when the cancer recurrs or reappears somewhere else. Further treatments will be undertaken and if well enough the child may return to school. If further relapses occur the disease usually progresses until the child dies. (See final part 'Facing the Death of a Child' for help and advice.)

Educational implications

Some children may be able to attend school between treatments and are therefore less likely to fall seriously behind with school work or lose touch with friends. However, for many children, returning to school after cancer treatment is a daunting experience. Changes in physical appearance can make them feel self-conscious, they may have lost touch with their former friends and classmates, they may feel that they will never 'catch up' with school work and they may well be facing emotional problems in coming to terms with the seriousness of their condition.

Peers and teachers may feel unsure and uncertain too. There may be many worries that they are afraid to voice and yet so many questions to ask.

It is therefore vital that issues such as 'How much does the child know?' and 'What do we tell the other children?' are addressed before the child returns to school.

Ideally the management of the child with cancer will be the result of joint planning by the medical team, the child (where appropriate), the family (parents/carers, extended family and siblings), and school and support staff. Specialist social workers and MacMillan nurses can be a source of help and support not only to the family but to school staff as well. Liaison between all involved with the child all the way through the illness, recovery and return to school, will eliminate, or at least lessen, potential problems. Ideally the child will not have lost touch with friends, classmates and teachers. Visits to the child in hospital or at home can keep friendships alive and reduce feelings of alienation and isolation. A structured programme of educational support while in hospital or via a home tutor can lessen anxiety about school work. Information will be needed from parents/medical staff about possible side effects to look out for, and a frank discussion about sensitive issues regarding the child's level of knowledge and understanding about the disease can prevent contradictory answers being given to the child and/or his or her peers. Where possible the child should be involved in decisions regarding how they would like information regarding their illness communicated to others (see 'Planning and preparation' - part 1).

While the child's return to school following treatment for cancer is a cause for celebration, it should be kept reasonably low-key. What most children want is to be able to slot back into school with minimum fuss, to be accepted by their friends and classmates, to get on with their work, and to be treated like everyone else.

(Information from Cancer Research Campaign in *Welcome Back!* Information also provided by Cancerlink)

What you can do

These are some of the ways you can help your pupil cope with school after treatment for cancer.

Above all, try to establish normality and set achievable goals, even for children with a poor outlook.

1. Visit the child in hospital, and perhaps bring along one or two classmates, if the child agrees. Keeping in touch will help the child to feel part of the class and be keen to get back to school again.

2. Discuss the basic medical facts about your specific child with a member of the hospital medical team, the hospital teacher, paediatric social worker or liaison sister. It is common policy for teachers to be contacted directly by a member of the hospital care team shortly after diagnosis. Rarely will the parents refuse permission.

3. Arrange to meet the parents before the child returns to school, to discuss any worries or potential problems the child might have on returning to school.

4. Ask the parents how much the child knows about the cancer, and how much information they would like you to pass on to others at the school. It might help to point out that all members of staff should know about the illness, and that classmates can be a great source of support when the child returns.

It is also important that you ask the child how much information he or she would like you to pass on, and to whom.

5. Try to meet the hospital teacher to discuss and hand over the schedule of work you have prepared for the child.

If the child is having home tuition, liaise with the home tutor and co-ordinate the schedule of school work to be done.

6. Check that the child will have easy access to classrooms, toilets, the dining room and playground. If necessary, try to arrange for the child to leave the class five minutes early to avoid the rush.

7. If the child has to remain inside during breaks and lunchtimes, organise any extra supervision that may be needed.

8. Be flexible about work. Most children who have had cancer are very keen to catch up and to sit the same examinations as their peers.

9. Try, where possible, to integrate the child's illness into classroom activities. Some children enjoy relating their experiences to the rest of the class. It is essential to ask the child first whether he or she would like this.

10. Teachers sometimes make the mistake of holding up children with cancer as 'good examples' to the rest of the school. This approach is unhelpful, can be divisive, and should be avoided.

11. If you teach the brother or sister of a child with cancer, arrange to meet the child's parents to find out what the sibling knows and feels about the illness. It is usually a good idea to encourage children to talk about their brother or sister who has cancer.

This page has been designed so that you can take photocopies and pass them to other teachers at the school.

Reproduced with kind permission from 'Welcome Back' Cancer Research Campaign.

A note about siblings

Having a child with cancer can sometimes create tensions within the family and between parents. Having a brother or sister with cancer can arouse strong and often conflicting emotions in the siblings. Jealousy and resentment are not uncommon because of the additional attention the sick child is receiving. This can lead to feelings of guilt and even in some cases a feeling that they, the brother or sister, are in some way responsible for their sibling's illness. Behavioural difficulties may occur in previously well-behaved, well-motivated children. If all staff in school are kept informed about the child with cancer in the family, these problems in the siblings can be dealt with sensitively and with understanding. Children should be encouraged to talk openly about their feelings to a trusted adult, and to be listened to in a non-judgemental way.

Childhood Heart Conditions

Description and treatment

One child in 100 is born with a congenital heart condition. The heart is formed during the first few weeks of pregnancy and in some cases it does not develop normally. It is becoming more common for heart conditions to be diagnosed before the baby is born, but most will be diagnosed at, or soon after birth. Some of these conditions are so minor that they require no treatment; some correct themselves, but about half will require surgery. There is a very wide range of congenital heart conditions which differ in degree and complexity. For some children with severe heart conditions corrective surgery may be carried out prior to the child starting school. Others will need periods of hospitalisation for treatment or surgery during the school years. In some the condition can be corrected by surgery, in others the function of the heart can be much improved. For some regular medication can relieve symptoms such as a build up of fluid in the body or danger of blood clots.

Educational implications

It is essential that a health care plan is drawn up (see Part 1) particularly for children with uncorrected heart conditions and that the advice of medical staff and parents is sought.

Children with uncorrected heart conditions

In school teachers should be aware of the following possible effects of the condition:

- the child may tire more quickly than other children

- s/he may become breathless more quickly

- lips and skin may become blue in some cases

- in others they might look a healthy pink

- they cannot keep up with their peers

- symptoms are usually worse in cold weather

Care is concerned with allowing the child to rest if breathless and/or blue, or very pale. The amount of exercise s/he takes may need to be limited. They will need to be allowed to stop when they feel it is necessary. They may need to stay in school in a warm place in cold weather.

- Some children have a very slow pulse rate which may cause them to faint.

- Some children have periods of very fast heart rate.

- It is very rare for a child to collapse in school.

In extreme cases parents may need to be called, or failing that a doctor or an ambulance. It is important to have an agreed procedure in place in case of emergencies.

Medication may need to be taken to reduce symptoms. For some children with heart conditions there is a build up of fluid in the body because the heart is not working efficiently. Medication can be taken to rid the body of these excess fluids but the effect will be that the child will need to go to the toilet more frequently and sometimes more urgently. Teachers need to be aware and to make allowances for this. For some children there is a risk of blood clots forming and a blood thinning medication (e.g. Warfarin) may be prescribed. It is important that these children avoid contact sports.

For most children, however, it is advised that they lead as near a normal life as possible.

Most children with a heart condition will undergo surgery at some time either in order to correct the defect, or to attempt to improve the condition and/or alleviate symptoms.

For children for whom a correction is possible considerable improvements can be noticed after surgery when children should be allowed to return to normal schooling. Some children will require a series of operations over a number of years and frequent hospitalisations. For these children the educational implications are more long-term (see Heart Conditions and Special Educational Needs).

Returning to school after heart surgery

Each child is an individual and should be treated as such. Children with the same condition react differently. Each child should be treated according to his/her own wishes and those of the parents.

Convalescence for most children undergoing heart surgery is quite quick and they will be able to return to school. For many the most noticeable effect will be that they look and feel much better. However some concerns may remain.

The child may be anxious about the reaction of classmates to his/her return to school; they may be worried about how much schooling they may have missed and how they will ever 'catch up'. They may have concerns about their involvement in games and PE and the general 'rough and tumble' of the school playground.

Teachers will have anxieties too that are not dissimilar to the child's. The best antidote to anxiety is to be prepared in advance. To allay the child's concerns about school work either the child's own teachers can send work home or into the hospital to be supervised by parents, or in some situations a hospital teacher or home-tutor can provide suitable work for the child to do when sufficiently recovered from the operation. Friends and classmates should be encouraged to visit the child to avoid feelings of isolation, or if this is not possible keeping in touch by letter or phone can be very reassuring.

Teachers should expect to receive information and advice about the child's condition from a medical practitioner prior to the child's return to school. They should consult with the parents for advice on how to handle the child's return, on how much physically the child is able to do and what and how much to tell the other children. If at all possible the child should be involved in these decisions.

If the heart condition is more complex, surgery may not be able to correct the defect. However it can be effective in improving and/or maintaining the condition. For these children there will not be such a marked improvement in their condition and convalescence may be more prolonged. Hospital or home tuition will be needed to keep the child motivated and to bring a degree of normality into their lives. Contact with home friends, peers and teachers is particularly important. On return to school many of the symptoms outlined above for children with untreated heart conditions may still pertain and it is very important to obtain further advice from parents and medical practitioners as to the likely consequences of only partially successful, or unsuccessful surgery. A new health care plan may need to be drawn up.

Children with heart conditions and special educational needs
Most children with heart conditions do not have special educational needs as part of the condition. Many of the educational implications such as poor concentration found in a child with an untreated heart condition as outlined above will improve after surgery. However, some children with heart conditions, as with other children with serious medical conditions, may experience special educational needs such as underachievement and low attainment as a result of prolonged absences from school and/or periods of ill-health, and some children with heart disorders do have associated long-term learning difficulties. For these children monitoring via the school-based stages of assessment as outlined in the DfEE's *Code of Practice* (1994) will need to be followed and for a few children a statutory assessment and a subsequent statement will be required (see Part 3).
(Information provided by Children's Heart Federation in *Information for Teachers*)
Some children with heart disorders have learning difficulties due to an associated disorder e.g. Down's syndrome. Most of these children are identified very early and will have a statement of special needs before school entry. Most will have moderate or severe learning difficulties.
A brief discussion of Down's syndrome appears at the end of this part on medical conditions. Readers who require more information are urged to contact the Down's Syndrome Association (address at the end of this book).

Down's Syndrome
Down's syndrome is primarily a learning difficulty and is not a medical condition in the sense that it is not an illness which requires 'treatment' or medication as with other conditions described in this book. However there are some medical and health problems which are more common among children with Down's syndrome which may require medical intervention which it is appropriate to discuss here. In addition children with Down's syndrome experience learning difficulties within the moderate to severe range.

Description

People with Down's syndrome have 47 instead of 46 chromosomes. They have an extra 21 chromosome in each cell. This is caused by a biological accident before birth, at or around the time of conception. This results in disruption of the growth of the developing embryo, and a degree of developmental delay in the child.

People with Down's syndrome often share a number of physical characteristics, which include:

- short stature

- eyes that look different - they slant upward and outward and the eyelids often have an extra fold of skin (epicanthic fold)

- small ears

- short fingers

- poor muscle tone

Possible health problems among children with Down's syndrome

Teachers and assistants who work with children with Down's syndrome should be aware that certain medical conditions are more common. These include:

- heart defects

- hearing loss

- visual difficulties

- gastrointestinal conditions

- poor muscle tone

Heart defects

About 40 per cent of children with Down's syndrome will also have a heart defect. The advice given in the previous chapter on heart conditions is equally applicable here. Some of these children will have to undergo surgery, some will need medication, all will require careful monitoring and close observation to make sure that they are allowed to rest when physical activity becomes too tiring, and that they are protected from extreme weather conditions.

Many children with Down's syndrome suffer from poor circulation even if they do not have a heart defect. They are prone to 'feel the cold' in winter and overheat in warm weather. Appropriate action needs to be taken.

Hearing loss

Children with Down's syndrome are particularly prone to colds which they find more difficult than most children to 'shake off'. The Eustacian tubes are particularly narrow giving rise to middle ear infections and sometimes 'glue ear' with subsequent hearing loss, which may be temporary, or more long term if untreated. Teachers and assistants should be aware of the likelihood of hearing problems in children with Down's syndrome, and the possible long-term effects upon speech, language and educational development. Medical and educational advice should be sought and strategies put into place to try to compensate for the hearing difficulties. (See *Spotlight on Special Educational Needs: Hearing Problems* for more detailed advice.)

Visual difficulties

Visual difficulties are less common than hearing problems in children with Down's syndrome but some children will need to wear glasses, and a few will have more serious visual impairments, some of which develop during childhood. Again teachers and assistants need to be aware of possible visual difficulties that might be present or that might develop in children with Down's syndrome and should take appropriate advice.

Gastrointestinal conditions

A small number of infants with Down's syndrome are born with malformations of the gastrointestinal tract. Despite early surgery a few of these children will experience a permanent difficulty in controlling their bowels. This may take the form of chronic constipation, or may lead to frequent soiling and the child may need to wear pads and need help with toileting. Trained assistance should be made available by the school or the LEA to cope with this problem and to minimise stigma or embarrassment to the child.

Poor muscle tone

Many babies with Down's syndrome tend to be 'floppy' (hypotonic) but this generally improves as the child grows. Teachers and assistants should be aware that as a result it will take longer for the child to acquire fine and

47

gross motor skills, therefore aspects of the PE curriculum, and writing and recording tasks may need to be modified until adequate skill levels are reached.

Poor muscle tone in the mouth and tongue can contribute to a delay in language development of the child with Down's syndrome. Difficulties can be experienced with the production of sounds required for talking clearly. The advice of a speech therapist can contribute towards strategies for improving language development.

Down's syndrome and special educational needs

Children with Down's syndrome have learning difficulties as described under the *1996 Education Act* and the *Code of Practice*. Therefore special educational provision will be required for them. Down's syndrome is usually diagnosed at the time of, or very soon after birth, and a statement of special educational needs will be produced before the child starts school, and in some cases much earlier.

Pre-school children can take advantage of mainstream or special nursery or playgroup provision and in some authorities home teaching schemes (such as Portage) may be available.

Children with Down's syndrome display a range of learning abilities and disabilities and education at school age requires careful planning and consultation between parents and professionals. In recent years there has been a move towards greater integration into mainstream schools for children with Down's syndrome, especially in the primary years. Successful integration relies heavily on the willingness of the school to make it work, and on the provision of adequate support for the school in the form of LEA Support Service involvement and additional staffing. Classroom assistance is usually required to meet the educational, social and medical needs of the child with Down's syndrome in mainstream schools. Some parents opt for special school provision especially if the child's learning difficulties are severe.

(Information provided by Down's Syndrome Association in *Information for Teachers*)

Part 5 – The support assistant and children with medical needs

The new thinking that children with serious medical needs can and should be educated in their mainstream schools where possible has contributed to the rise in the employment of additional 'non-teaching' staff.

It can be seen in earlier chapters in this book that pupils with serious medical needs do not necessarily have special educational needs i.e. learning difficulties, and many of the children learn at a young age how to cope with various aspects of their own medical care.

However in some cases the employment of a classroom assistant can contribute significantly to the successful integration of the pupil, to their general welfare and safety and to the particular medical care needed to keep the pupil well and safe. In a busy mainstream classroom the presence of a second adult can significantly raise the classteacher's perception of his/her ability to cope and potential anxiety can be lessened.

The reasons for the employment of an assistant for a child with a medical condition are:

- to assist with the integration of children with medical needs especially on entry to school to promote a positive attitude and to allay anxiety on the part of parents and school staff (this support may be withdrawn as confidence increases)

- to assist with specific medical procedures that need to be carried out regularly, sometimes daily, e.g. physiotherapy for a child with cystic fibrosis

- to support some aspects of the curriculum which are potentially risky for some children e.g. PE/games and swimming for children with epilepsy

- to support the re-entry of children following surgery and/or prolonged absence from school

- to support any learning difficulties that might arise from such an absence

- to support any learning difficulties that might arise because of the condition e.g. Down's syndrome

- to implement specific targets on an individual education plan

- to provide supervision for children unable to take part in extra-curricula activities such as playtimes and outdoor games sessions e.g. children with serious heart conditions in winter months.

There may well be other duties that can be carried out by assistants. What is important is that s/he has a clear job description, that adequate training is provided, and that s/he is included in initial and subsequent planning meetings, setting up of a health care plan and invited to reviews.

Some LEAs put on training courses especially focused at classroom support assistants; some schools, clusters or pyramids of schools do the same.

With the increased use of classroom assistants in mainstream schools a number of training packages have been published and are listed at the back of this book. Some (OPTIS and SAINTS for example) have 'core' material or induction packages, and then specialist packages, some of which might be adapted to be relevant to an assistant supporting a child with a serious medical condition.

Probably the best training for such a person would come from medical and paramedical staff and the *child's parents*, as needs are very individual in most cases.

Balshaw (1991) outlines six principles through which schools can review their policy and practice in relation to classroom assistants which are also relevant in this context.

1. 'Roles and responsibilities - classroom assistants should be clear about their roles and responsibilities
2. Communication - classroom assistants should understand the communication system of the school
3. Consistency of approach - classroom assistants should be seen positively as part of the provision to meet children's needs
4. A working team - classroom assistants should be part of a working team
5. Using personal skills - classroom assistants should be encouraged to make use of their personal skills
6. Staff development needs - classroom assistants should be helped to develop their personal and professional skills alongside other members of staff.'

Classroom assistants can become very close to individual children they support. This may have positive and potentially negative outcomes. On the positive side the assistant becomes the friend and confidante of the child and may be the first to notice or learn about potential problems. However if this relationship is too close the child may become too dependent, it may cut across the child's social relationships with other children, and may become oppressive and stultifying. The advice printed below could apply to any classroom assistant but seems particularly relevant to one supporting a child with a serious medical need.

REMEMBER

- Behave towards the pupil as you would to any other pupil of the same age

- Maintain a balance between giving support and promoting independence

- Maintain the child's dignity and protect his/her right to privacy

- Keep a low profile; some pupils do not like being singled out by the 'attachment' of a member of staff

- Keep expectations and standards high

- Actively promote self-confidence and a high self-esteem

- Ask for help and advice when you need it; don't struggle on your own

- Working with pupils with special needs (special medical needs) can sometimes be upsetting and stressful. Discussing your worries with another adult in the school is in no way a sign of failure, but is positive and beneficial to all concerned

Part 6 – The family

Throughout this book the importance of parental involvement at all stages of their child's education has been stressed. Schools should be seen as working in partnership with parents, and parents, of necessity, become very knowledgeable about their child's condition. In the chapter about childhood cancers the situation with regard to siblings was raised and some issues were discussed.

Inevitably having a child with any serious medical condition will affect all members of that family; parents, siblings and extended family. Even if the condition is not 'life-threatening' in the accepted sense, and is well controlled, anxiety about the child's well-being, safety at school, academic progress and relationships with teachers and peers can lead to an (apparently) unusually protective reaction by family members, and sometimes can alter the family dynamics in an unexpected way. In some cases, for example cystic fibrosis, the round of medication, physiotherapy, hospital appointments and disturbed nights can lead to exhaustion of the parents/carers and feelings of isolation and alienation. If the condition is life-threatening or indeed terminal the situation within the family will become even more stressful.

How do these stresses manifest themselves in the family members and how can schools help?

The nature and stage of the child's condition will produce different reactions. At diagnosis parents are naturally shocked and experience grief and anxiety especially if the condition is chronic, life-threatening or inherited. Parents who are worried or anxious can appear aggressive and over-protective to hard-pressed teachers, who may themselves be having some difficulty coming to terms with the diagnosis and its implications for life at school. Teachers should try to understand the reactions of parents and display a calm, confident yet sympathetic response.

It is important to emphasise to parents that their child is a welcome and valued member of the school; that they will have access to all aspects of the curriculum and extra-curricular activities wherever possible; that parents will be involved as active partners in their child's education and kept informed and their advice sought and valued at all times.

For the siblings, their age, position in the family and relationships within it are all factors that will have a bearing on how they cope. Teachers should be made aware of the situation at home, and be prepared for reactions from siblings. Feelings of guilt, resentment, isolation and insecurity are common, in addition to worry and the anxiety of the possibility of becoming sick themselves. These feelings are unlikely to manifest themselves in an obvious way and school staff should look out for a drop in the level of motivation and achievement of the sibling, poor attention and concentration, day-dreaming and tiredness. Sometimes attention-seeking behaviour can erupt in a previously well-behaved pupil - the 'what about me?' syndrome, or the pupil can become quiet and withdrawn.

A classroom ethos which encourages the expression of feelings through circle-time or personal and social education can do much to help the troubled sibling talk about his/her fears in a supportive atmosphere. In some cases s/he may seek out another child or a trusted adult. Any anxiety on the part of the school about siblings should be discussed with parents. It may be that the parents are so involved in the care of the sick child that the needs of brothers and sisters can, inadvertently, be overlooked. Teachers will need to show understanding and concern for all members of the family.

Part 7 – Facing the death of a child

It is fortunately rare, but it does happen, that a child with a serious medical condition can die as a result of the condition or of complications associated with it. It is exceedingly rare for the child to die in school, unexpectedly, but even if the child dies in hospital or at home, their death is likely to have a profound impact on the staff and pupils of that school.

There are articles in journals which deal with the care of the dying child, his/her siblings and parents, but little seems to be available on how a school and the children and staff in it prepare for and cope with the death of one of its pupils. This chapter seeks to look at ways schools and headteachers in particular can prepare staff and children in advance for the death of a pupil; the impact on the child's siblings; support the school can offer to the bereaved family, and how to cope in the aftermath of a death by celebrating the life of the child and keeping the memories alive. The key would seem to be planning ahead even at a time when no child or adult in the school is seriously ill or dying.

The planning ahead can take two forms. Firstly planning for 'death education' to be part of the curriculum, formal and informal, and secondly for all schools to have developed a contingency plan to cope with crises in school.

Keeping death alive

No-one, no headteacher or member of staff, really anticipates that they will have to deal with the death of a pupil, and indeed many will never have to, and yet many children experience death in their lives outside school.

Therefore it is important that an atmosphere of openness in talking about feelings in general is encouraged via circle time or through the PSE curriculum. The subject of death and dying may need to be introduced into these sessions so that when a situation occurs the staff and children have already climbed the first hurdle and brought this 'taboo' subject out into the open, and the teacher has signalled that it is as all right to talk about death as it is to talk about birth. An atmosphere of openness and acceptance in talking about death and dying needs to be fostered in all schools. It has been suggested that all schools should address the issue of death and dying at least once a term either through PSE lessons or through story which may stimulate discussion. (A selection of suitable stories is printed at the end of this book.)

Most children have to face bereavement of one sort or another at some time during their school career. For some their first experience of death may be that of a beloved pet and their feelings of grief should be respected and listened to. Sometimes the death is of an elderly relative or grandparent, but occasionally a parent or a sibling, and being able to talk about their feelings to a trusted adult in school can help the process of grieving. For older children 'death education' may form part of the religious education or religious studies syllabus. The term 'death education' refers to dealing with death in all its aspects within the school curriculum. In her book *Death in the Classroom*, Gatliffe (1988) identifies four goals in introducing this topic into schools. They include: informing pupils of, and helping them to understand, the facts of death and dying, and the many beliefs and practices concerning death and beyond death. Although this topic may not be on the syllabus for all schools a study of this subject would enable teachers and pupils alike to confront this very difficult and challenging aspect of life.

Coping with crises in school

Schools often have to cope with crises. Sometimes they seem comparatively minor - a flu epidemic in which more than half the staff are affected; a flood in the boys' toilets; a break-in at night; - the list is endless, but these are crises that are faced and dealt with as part of the school routine.

Sometimes the traumas are more major - a serious fire; a violent physical assault on a teacher; the expulsion of a number of pupils for drug dealing. And sometimes school children get caught up in major disasters such as Aberfan and Dunblane. However closely or otherwise individuals are involved in major traumas or disasters, and regardless of the size of the incident, the distress caused can be devastating at the time and have long-term repercussions.

It is suggested (Yule and Gould, 1993) that thinking ahead and forward planning may help a school cope better at the time of the crisis and reduce the distress and after-effects of staff and pupils. They suggest that all schools should have a contingency plan that can be activated at times of crisis.

This contingency plan might include: identifying potential crises; collating a list of significant contacts and telephone numbers; and actions planned and responsibilities apportioned so that in the case of a crisis the action plan can be activated with minimum delay.

There is not space in this publication to explore this topic further. Readers will find the book *Wise Before the Event* (Yule and Gould, 1993) practical, straightforward and concise.

A major crisis in any school would be the death of one of its pupils.

The death of a pupil

Throughout this book importance has been placed on the need for schools to be in continuous close contact with the family of a child with a serious medical condition, and on the need to be aware of how much the child knows and understands about their condition. Where the illness is known to be life-threatening and moves into a terminal phase the importance of the above advice cannot be over-emphasised. As the child's death approaches and when they do die it is important to work with the parents and to try to do whatever they want.

Preparation

- It is important to continue to visit the dying child for as long as possible, if that is what s/he and the parents want, although it is common for the child not to want to see anyone except close family in the few days before death.

- Talk to others who have been through a similar experience and adapt their advice to your own particular circumstances.

- Contact support staff or agencies known. Often there is a member of the hospital staff who can lend support and practical help.

- It is probably not possible to prepare the children in advance for the death of one of their fellow pupils. It is likely that they will know that the child is seriously ill, and that special prayers may have been said or quiet moments may have been kept for the child.

- Prepare staff by talking about the child and the imminent death. Staff should be free to express their own feelings. Be practical, however hard that may be and decide on a plan of action. Decide in advance what will be done and by whom. Decisions need to be made about who will tell the other pupils. Should this be done in a whole school assembly or each teacher to tell their own class or form group? What about special and close friends - should they be told separately and by whom?

- The headteacher might prepare in advance a letter to the child's parents and a letter to the parents of the other children.

- Decisions need to be made about what to do with the child's belongings at school - contents of the child's drawer, pens, pencils etc.

55

If these preparations are made in advance of the child's death it will leave staff freer to deal with their own and the pupils' feelings of grief.

After the child has died the action plan that has already been decided upon can be brought into action and the children, other parents and members of staff told. The affected class will feel the grief most deeply and for longer, especially close friends. They should be told separately from the rest of the class.

Children will react in different ways. Very young children may not initially react very much at all. Older children may ask questions like 'Why couldn't the doctors make him better?' 'Where is she now?' Questions should be answered as honestly as possible. Some children may need permission to cry and school staff should not be afraid of letting the children see them cry too.

School staff should continue to work closely with the parents and make sure that they are kept informed about how the school collectively would like to respond. Decisions need to be made in consultation with the parents as to who will attend the funeral and what form the school's memorial will take. A service to celebrate the life of the child could be held at a later date to which parents and the child's family could be invited.

Many children will want to make their own individual response. They may want to write letters or poems, make cards or draw pictures or bring flowers.

A central point, a table in the hall for example, might be set aside for individual contributions that can be displayed and later collected to send to the family.

It is likely that in the weeks following the child's death the academic work of those very close to the child will suffer. Mood swings are common and the level of concentration will fluctuate. Siblings of the child are likely to be more profoundly affected and as outlined in a previous chapter may take an unexpected form. Staff too may find it difficult to come to terms with the child's death and a supportive staff room will help here. Of particular concern is support for the headteacher who is likely to have had to bear the lion's share of organisation and support for children, staff and parents. It is important to remember that the process of bereavement can take up to three years to go through.

Some fitting memorial to the child should be negotiated with the parents. This might take the form of a bench in the playground, a tree in the grounds or a photograph of the child within the school building where it can be seen by all the school population.

A comprehensive list of stories, reference books, and articles concerning death and bereavement appears at the end of this book.

Part 8 – Useful Addresses

The author and publishers are grateful to the following organisations for their help and support in the writing of this book.

All these organisations publish information packs, booklets and leaflets which give more detailed information than can be included here. Readers are urged to contact them if further help or information is required.

Diabetes
British Diabetic Association
10 Queen Anne Street
London
W1M 0BD
Tel: 0171 323 1531

Epilepsy
British Epilepsy Association
Anstey House
40 Hanover Square
Leeds
LS3 1BE
Tel: 0113 243 9393
Helpline: (Freephone) 0800 30 90 30

National Society for Epilepsy
Chalfont St Peter
Gerrards Cross
Bucks
SL9 0RJ
Tel: 01494 601300
Helpline: 01494 601400

Cystic Fibrosis
Cystic Fibrosis Trust
Alexandra House
5 Blyth Road
Bromley
Kent
BR1 3RS
Tel: 0181 464 7211

Asthma
National Asthma Campaign
Providence House
Providence Place
London
N1 0NT
Tel: 0171 226 2260
Helpline: 0345 01 02 03

Childhood Cancers
Cancerlink
11-21 Northdown Street
London
N1 9BN
Tel: 0172 833 4963
Helpline: (Freephone) 0800 132905

Cancer Research Campaign
10 Cambridge Terrace
London
NW1 4JL
Tel: 0171 224 1333

ME
Action for ME and Chronic Fatigue
P.O. Box 1302
Wells, BA5 2WE
Tel: 01749 670799

Heart Conditions
Children's Heart Federation
115 Gloucester Place
London W1H 3PJ
Tel: 0171 935 4737

Down's Syndrome
Down's Syndrome Association
155 Mitcham Road
London SW17 9PG
Tel: 0181 682 4001

Other Useful Addresses

Carers National Association
20-25 Glasshouse Yard
London EC1 4JS
Tel: 0171 490 8898

Compassionate Friends (Bereavement)
53 North Street
Bristol BS3 1EN
Tel: 01272 539639

Contact-A-Family
170 Tottenham Court Road
London
W1P 0HA
Tel: 0171 383 3555

CRUSE (bereavement care)
Cruse House
126 Sheen Road
Richmond
Surrey
TW9 1UR
Tel: 0181 940 4841
(helpline - 0181 332 7227)

Department of Health (Health Information Service)
Richmond House
79 Whitehall
London
SW1 2NS
Tel: 0800 665544

Eating Disorders Association
Sackville Place
44 Magdalen Street
Norwich
Norfolk NR3 1JU
Tel: 01603 621414

National Association for the Education of Sick Children
St Margarets House
17 Old Ford Road
London
E2 9PL
Tel: 0181 980 8523

National Eczema Society
4 Tavistock Place
London
WC1H 9RA
Tel: 0171 388 4097

National Kidney Patients Association/Federation
6 Stanley Street
Worksop
Notts
S81 7HX
Tel: 01909 487795

National Meningitis Trust
Fern House
Bath Road
Stroud
Glos
GL5 3TJ
Tel: 01453 755049 (helpline - 24hrs)

National Standing Conference of Hospital Teachers
145 Hardham Road
Pailton-le-Fylde
Lancs
FY6 8ES
Tel: 01253 891928

Further Reading

Marsh, H, Partridge, L and Youngs, C (1995) Editors
The CAF Directory of Specific Conditions and Rare Syndromes in Children with their Family Networks.
    The directory provides brief information about a range of specific conditions and syndromes in easily accessible form. As a resource to parents it puts them in touch with others who have been through the same experience.

On Death and Bereavement

Abrams, R (1992)
Bereaved and Bewildered in Times Educational Supplement: October 1992.

Abrams, R (1992)
When Parents Die. Letts: London.
    The author wrote this article and subsequent book following the unexpected deaths of her father and then stepfather when she was still in her teens. Drawing on her personal experience she suggests that pre-emptive, rather than reactive, measures on the part of teachers can go a long way to minimise the grief and pain felt by bereaved youngsters.

Ball, M (1976)
Death (A 'Standpoint' Book). Oxford University Press: Oxford.
    This book attempts to open up this 'taboo' subject from the author's 'standpoint'. It aims to give a basis for thought and discussion and probes the inward and outward reactions of people to death, grief and mourning.

Chadwick, A (1994)
Living With Grief in School. Family Reading Centre Ltd: Kent.
    A practical guide for primary school staff covering such issues as teaching opportunities, concepts of death in society and in young children, and the death of a pupil or staff member.

Drought, B (1996)
Life in the Shadow of Death in Times Educational Supplement: 17 May 1996.
    An article which explores ways in which teachers can help children whose siblings are suffering from a terminal illness.

Gatliffe, E (1988)
Death in the Classroom. Epworth Press: London.
This book offers a realistic curriculum for 'death education' and opens up many ways into the subject which allows children to explore their feelings about death without putting undue pressure on them to do so.

Machin, L and Holt, C (1988)
All Change. Christian Education Movement: Iselworth, Middlesex.
A resource book for teachers of older children which, through a series of pictures and stories, explores feelings of loss, separation and death. Teachers/leaders notes give advice on how the material might be used, but is not in any way prescriptive.

Wynnejones, P (1985)
Children, Death and Bereavement. Scripture Union: Trinity Press Worcester.
The author has drawn together material from a variety of sources and aims to help adults talk with children about death in a natural and positive way.

Story Books for Children about Death and Parting
Alex, M and B (1981)
Grandpa and Me. Lion Publishing: Tring, Herts.
This is the story of Emma and her first encounters with death - first her kitten and then the death of her Grandpa. A story told from a Christian perspective.

Anholt, L (1995)
The Magpie Song. Heinemann: London.
This story explores the warm relationship between a young girl and her elderly grandfather through an exchange of letters - and the secrets they share even after his death.

Bowen, S (1995)
Laura's Granny. Scripture Union: Trinity Press Worcester.
A story from a Christian perspective in which Laura learns how to say goodbye when her much loved granny dies.

Schindler, R (1989)
Ben and the New Life. St Paul Publications: Slough.
Ben's friend Tommy dies, and after the sadness and grief Ben begins to understand a hope for Tommy in a 'new life.' Another simple story told from a Christian perspective.

Simmonds, P (1987)
Fred. Penguin Books: London.
   A picture story which explores the death - and celebration of the life - of Fred, Sophie and Nick's aged cat.

Stilz, C C (1989)
Kirsty's Kite. Lion Publishing: Tring, Herts.
   Kirsty's mother has died and she is left in the care of her Grandad. Grandad buys her a beautiful kite and as she flies it and talks to him she is able to face her mother's death and find the reassurance she needs.

Varley, S (1984)
Badger's Parting Gift. Anderson Press: London.
   During his life Badger gave each of his friends a simple gift - something he had taught them that they could now do well. It is through their shared memories of him that they begin to come to terms with his death.

Wilhelm, H (1985)
I'll Always Love You. Hodder and Stoughton: London.
   A picture book which sensitively portrays the close relationship between a boy and his dog, Elfie. When the dog dies, although grief-stricken he takes comfort in the fact that every night he told Elfie, 'I'll always love you.'

Dealing with crises in school
Yule, W and Gould, A (1993)
Wise Before the Event. Gulbenkian Foundation: London.
   Disasters do happen and sometimes their victims are school children: consequently the schools they attend may be affected in a number of ways. The purpose of this practical little book is to raise awareness of the possible effects of disasters on children, and to suggest ways in which advance planning can reduce their impact.

References

Balshaw, M H (1991) *Help in the Classroom.* David Fulton Publishers: London.

Beveridge, S (1996) *Spotlight on Special Educational Needs: Learning Difficulties.* NASEN Publications: Tamworth.

Colby, J (1996) in *Special Children, May 1966.* Questions Publishing Co: Buxton.

Department for Education (1994) *Code of Practice on the Identification and Assessment of Special Educational Needs.*

Department for Education and Employment (1993) *The Education Act.*

Department for Education (1994) *Education of Sick Children (Circular 12/94).*

Department for Education and Employment (1996) *Supporting Pupils with Medical Needs.*

Department of Education and Science (1978) *Special Educational Needs: Report of the Committee of Enquiry into the Education of Handicapped Children and Young People (Warnock Report).* Her Majesty's Stationary Office: London.

Gatliffe, E (1988) *Death in the Classroom.* Epworth Press: London.

Ho Yen, D (1995) *British Journal of Psychiatry vol 116* in Colby (1996).

Mason, M (1995) *Spotlight on Special Educational Needs: Visual Impairment.* NASEN Publications: Tamworth.

Oxfordshire County Council and Bedfordshire County Council (1992) *Helping in School. OPTIS.* Cowley: Oxford.

Watson, L (1996) Spotlight on Special Educational Needs: Hearing Impairment. NASEN Publications: Tamworth.

Wiltshire County Council. *SAIL - Support Assistant's Induction Log.*

Yule, W and Gould, A (1993) *Wise Before the Event.* Gulbenkian Foundation: London.